wellness diary

—

Eat Well, Live Well, Enjoy Life

Supplements/Medications

_____

How many servings of vegetables did you eat today?

_____

How many glasses of water did you drink today?

_____

Exercise:

_____

_____

Mindfulness & Meditation:

_____

_____

Personal Activities:

_____

_____

What 3 things are you grateful for today?

1._____

2._____

3._____

What could you have done better today?

_____

_____

_____

DATE: /   / 20

How are you feeling today?

Urgh   OK   Good   Fantastic

How did you sleep last night?

_____

Breakfast   *Time*_____

*Food*_____

_____

*Drinks*_____

Lunch   *Time*_____

*Food*_____

_____

*Drinks*_____

Dinner   *Time*_____

*Food*_____

_____

*Drinks*_____

Snacks   *Time*_____

*Food*_____

_____

*Drinks*_____

Supplements/Medications

How many servings of vegetables did you eat today?

How many glasses of water did you drink today?

Exercise:

Mindfulness & Meditation:

Personal Activities:

What 3 things are you grateful for today?

1. _____
2. _____
3. _____

What could you have done better today?

DATE: / / 20

How are you feeling today?

Urgh   OK   Good   Fantastic

How did you sleep last night?

_____

Breakfast   *Time*_____
*Food*_____
_____
*Drinks*_____

Lunch   *Time*_____
*Food*_____
_____
*Drinks*_____

Dinner   *Time*_____
*Food*_____
_____
*Drinks*_____

Snacks   *Time*_____
*Food*_____
_____
*Drinks*_____

Supplements/Medications

How many servings of vegetables did you eat today?

How many glasses of water did you drink today?

Exercise:

Mindfulness & Meditation:

Personal Activities:

What 3 things are you grateful for today?

1.

2.

3.

What could you have done better today?

DATE: / / 20

How are you feeling today?

Urgh   OK   Good   Fantastic

How did you sleep last night?

_____

Breakfast   *Time*_____

*Food*_____

_____

_____

*Drinks*_____

Lunch   *Time*_____

*Food*_____

_____

_____

*Drinks*_____

Dinner   *Time*_____

*Food*_____

_____

_____

*Drinks*_____

Snacks   *Time*_____

*Food*_____

_____

_____

*Drinks*_____

Supplements/Medications

How many servings of vegetables did you eat today?

How many glasses of water did you drink today?

Exercise:

Mindfulness & Meditation:

Personal Activities:

What 3 things are you grateful for today?

1. _____

2. _____

3. _____

What could you have done better today?

DATE: / / 20

How are you feeling today?

Urgh   *OK*   *Good*   *Fantastic*

How did you sleep last night?

_____

Breakfast   *Time*_____

*Food*_____

_____

*Drinks*_____

Lunch   *Time*_____

*Food*_____

_____

*Drinks*_____

Dinner   *Time*_____

*Food*_____

_____

*Drinks*_____

Snacks   *Time*_____

*Food*_____

_____

*Drinks*_____

Supplements/Medications

_____

How many servings of vegetables did you eat today?

_____

How many glasses of water did you drink today?

_____

Exercise:

_____

_____

Mindfulness & Meditation:

_____

_____

Personal Activities:

_____

_____

What 3 things are you grateful for today?

1._____
2._____
3._____

What could you have done better today?

_____

_____

_____

DATE: /   / 20

How are you feeling today?

Urgh   OK   Good   Fantastic

How did you sleep last night?

_____

Breakfast   *Time*_____

*Food*_____

_____

_____

*Drinks*_____

Lunch   *Time*_____

*Food*_____

_____

_____

*Drinks*_____

Dinner   *Time*_____

*Food*_____

_____

_____

*Drinks*_____

Snacks   *Time*_____

*Food*_____

_____

_____

*Drinks*_____

Supplements/Medications

How many servings of vegetables did you eat today?

How many glasses of water did you drink today?

Exercise:

Mindfulness & Meditation:

Personal Activities:

What 3 things are you grateful for today?

1.
2.
3.

What could you have done better today?

DATE: /   / 20

How are you feeling today?

         Urgh   OK   Good   Fantastic

How did you sleep last night?

_____

Breakfast   *Time_____*

Food_____

_____

Drinks_____

Lunch   *Time_____*

Food_____

_____

Drinks_____

Dinner   *Time_____*

Food_____

_____

Drinks_____

Snacks   *Time_____*

Food_____

_____

Drinks_____

Supplements/Medications

_____

How many servings of vegetables did you eat today?

_____

How many glasses of water did you drink today?

_____

Exercise:

_____

_____

Mindfulness & Meditation:

_____

_____

Personal Activities:

_____

_____

What 3 things are you grateful for today?

1._____

2._____

3._____

What could you have done better today?

_____

_____

_____

DATE: /   / 20

How are you feeling today?

     Urgh OK Good Fantastic

How did you sleep last night?

_____

Breakfast *Time_____*

Food_____

_____

_____

Drinks_____

Lunch   *Time_____*

Food_____

_____

_____

Drinks_____

Dinner   *Time_____*

Food_____

_____

_____

Drinks_____

Snacks   *Time_____*

Food_____

_____

_____

Drinks_____

Supplements/Medications

_____

How many servings of vegetables did you eat today?

_____

How many glasses of water did you drink today?

_____

Exercise:

_____

_____

Mindfulness & Meditation:

_____

_____

Personal Activities:

_____

_____

What 3 things are you grateful for today?

1._____

2._____

3._____

What could you have done better today?

_____

_____

_____

DATE: / / 20

How are you feeling today?
Urgh   OK   Good   Fantastic

How did you sleep last night?
_____

Breakfast   *Time*_____
*Food*_____
_____
_____
*Drinks*_____

Lunch   *Time*_____
*Food*_____
_____
_____
*Drinks*_____

Dinner   *Time*_____
*Food*_____
_____
_____
*Drinks*_____

Snacks   *Time*_____
*Food*_____
_____
_____
*Drinks*_____

Supplements/Medications

_____

How many servings of vegetables did you eat today?

_____

How many glasses of water did you drink today?

_____

Exercise:

_____

_____

Mindfulness & Meditation:

_____

_____

Personal Activities:

_____

_____

What 3 things are you grateful for today?

1._____

2._____

3._____

What could you have done better today?

_____

_____

_____

DATE: / / 20

How are you feeling today?

Urgh   OK   Good   Fantastic

How did you sleep last night?

_____

Breakfast   *Time_____*

Food_____

_____

_____

Drinks_____

Lunch   *Time_____*

Food_____

_____

_____

Drinks_____

Dinner   *Time_____*

Food_____

_____

_____

Drinks_____

Snacks   *Time_____*

Food_____

_____

_____

Drinks_____

Supplements/Medications

_____

How many servings of vegetables did you eat today?

_____

How many glasses of water did you drink today?

_____

Exercise:

_____

_____

Mindfulness & Meditation:

_____

_____

Personal Activities:

_____

_____

What 3 things are you grateful for today?

1._____

2._____

3._____

What could you have done better today?

_____

_____

_____

DATE: /   / 20

How are you feeling today?

        Urgh   *OK*   *Good*   *Fantastic*

How did you sleep last night?

_____

Breakfast   *Time_____*

Food_____

_____

Drinks_____

Lunch   *Time_____*

Food_____

_____

Drinks_____

Dinner   *Time_____*

Food_____

_____

Drinks_____

Snacks   *Time_____*

Food_____

_____

Drinks_____

Supplements/Medications

_____

How many servings of vegetables did you eat today?

_____

How many glasses of water did you drink today?

_____

Exercise:

_____

_____

Mindfulness & Meditation:

_____

_____

Personal Activities:

_____

_____

What 3 things are you grateful for today?

1._____

2._____

3._____

What could you have done better today?

_____

_____

_____

DATE: /   / 20

How are you feeling today?

                Urgh   *OK*   *Good*   *Fantastic*

How did you sleep last night?

_____

Breakfast   *Time_____*

Food_____

_____

Drinks_____

Lunch   *Time_____*

Food_____

_____

Drinks_____

Dinner   *Time_____*

Food_____

_____

Drinks_____

Snacks   *Time_____*

Food_____

_____

Drinks_____

Supplements/Medications

How many servings of vegetables did you eat today?

How many glasses of water did you drink today?

Exercise:

Mindfulness & Meditation:

Personal Activities:

What 3 things are you grateful for today?

1.
2.
3.

What could you have done better today?

How are you feeling today?

        Urgh   *OK*   *Good*   *Fantastic*

How did you sleep last night?

_____

Breakfast   *Time_____*

Food_____

_____

Drinks_____

Lunch   *Time_____*

Food_____

_____

Drinks_____

Dinner   *Time_____*

Food_____

_____

Drinks_____

Snacks   *Time_____*

Food_____

_____

Drinks_____

Supplements/Medications

_____

How many servings of vegetables did you eat today?

_____

How many glasses of water did you drink today?

_____

Exercise:

_____

_____

Mindfulness & Meditation:

_____

_____

Personal Activities:

_____

_____

What 3 things are you grateful for today?

1._____

2._____

3._____

What could you have done better today?

_____

_____

_____

DATE: /   / 20

How are you feeling today?

Urgh   OK   Good   Fantastic

How did you sleep last night?

_____

Breakfast   *Time*_____
*Food*_____
_____
_____
*Drinks*_____

Lunch   *Time*_____
*Food*_____
_____
_____
*Drinks*_____

Dinner   *Time*_____
*Food*_____
_____
_____
*Drinks*_____

Snacks   *Time*_____
*Food*_____
_____
_____
*Drinks*_____

Supplements/Medications

_____

How many servings of vegetables did you eat today?

_____

How many glasses of water did you drink today?

_____

Exercise:

_____

_____

Mindfulness & Meditation:

_____

_____

Personal Activities:

_____

_____

What 3 things are you grateful for today?

1._____

2._____

3._____

What could you have done better today?

_____

_____

_____

DATE: / / 20

How are you feeling today?

Urgh   OK   Good   Fantastic

How did you sleep last night?

_____

Breakfast   *Time_____*

Food_____

_____

_____

Drinks_____

Lunch   *Time_____*

Food_____

_____

_____

Drinks_____

Dinner   *Time_____*

Food_____

_____

_____

Drinks_____

Snacks   *Time_____*

Food_____

_____

_____

Drinks_____

Supplements/Medications

_____

How many servings of vegetables did you eat today?

_____

How many glasses of water did you drink today?

_____

Exercise:

_____

_____

Mindfulness & Meditation:

_____

_____

Personal Activities:

_____

_____

What 3 things are you grateful for today?

1._____
2._____
3._____

What could you have done better today?

_____

_____

_____

How are you feeling today?

                Urgh   *OK*   *Good*   *Fantastic*

How did you sleep last night?

_____

Breakfast   *Time_____*

Food_____

_____

Drinks_____

Lunch   *Time_____*

Food_____

_____

Drinks_____

Dinner   *Time_____*

Food_____

_____

Drinks_____

Snacks   *Time_____*

Food_____

_____

Drinks_____

Supplements/Medications

_____

How many servings of vegetables did you eat today?

_____

How many glasses of water did you drink today?

_____

Exercise:

_____

_____

Mindfulness & Meditation:

_____

_____

Personal Activities:

_____

_____

What 3 things are you grateful for today?

1._____

2._____

3._____

What could you have done better today?

_____

_____

_____

DATE: /   / 20

How are you feeling today?

Urgh   OK   Good   Fantastic

How did you sleep last night?

_____

Breakfast   *Time_____*

Food_____

_____

_____

Drinks_____

Lunch   *Time_____*

Food_____

_____

_____

Drinks_____

Dinner   *Time_____*

Food_____

_____

_____

Drinks_____

Snacks   *Time_____*

Food_____

_____

_____

Drinks_____

Supplements/Medications

How many servings of vegetables did you eat today?

How many glasses of water did you drink today?

Exercise:

Mindfulness & Meditation:

Personal Activities:

What 3 things are you grateful for today?

1.

2.

3.

What could you have done better today?

DATE: /   / 20

How are you feeling today?

               Urgh   *OK*   *Good*   *Fantastic*

How did you sleep last night?

_____

Breakfast   *Time_____*

Food_____

_____

_____

Drinks_____

Lunch   *Time_____*

Food_____

_____

_____

Drinks_____

Dinner   *Time_____*

Food_____

_____

_____

Drinks_____

Snacks   *Time_____*

Food_____

_____

_____

Drinks_____

Supplements/Medications

How many servings of vegetables did you eat today?

How many glasses of water did you drink today?

Exercise:

Mindfulness & Meditation:

Personal Activities:

What 3 things are you grateful for today?

1.

2.

3.

What could you have done better today?

DATE: /   / 20

How are you feeling today?

Urgh   OK   Good   Fantastic

How did you sleep last night?

_____

Breakfast   *Time_____*

Food_____

_____

_____

Drinks_____

Lunch   *Time_____*

Food_____

_____

_____

Drinks_____

Dinner   *Time_____*

Food_____

_____

_____

Drinks_____

Snacks   *Time_____*

Food_____

_____

_____

Drinks_____

Supplements/Medications

_____

How many servings of vegetables did you eat today?

_____

How many glasses of water did you drink today?

_____

Exercise:

_____

_____

Mindfulness & Meditation:

_____

_____

Personal Activities:

_____

_____

What 3 things are you grateful for today?

1._____

2._____

3._____

What could you have done better today?

_____

_____

_____

DATE: /   / 20

How are you feeling today?

         Urgh   *OK*   *Good*   *Fantastic*

How did you sleep last night?

_____

Breakfast   *Time_____*

Food_____

_____

Drinks_____

Lunch   *Time_____*

Food_____

_____

Drinks_____

Dinner   *Time_____*

Food_____

_____

Drinks_____

Snacks   *Time_____*

Food_____

_____

Drinks_____

Supplements/Medications

_____

How many servings of vegetables did you eat today?

_____

How many glasses of water did you drink today?

_____

Exercise:

_____

_____

Mindfulness & Meditation:

_____

_____

Personal Activities:

_____

_____

What 3 things are you grateful for today?

1._____

2._____

3._____

What could you have done better today?

_____

_____

_____

DATE: /   / 20

How are you feeling today?

Urgh   OK   Good   Fantastic

How did you sleep last night?

_____

Breakfast   *Time_____*

Food_____

_____

Drinks_____

Lunch   *Time_____*

Food_____

_____

Drinks_____

Dinner   *Time_____*

Food_____

_____

Drinks_____

Snacks   *Time_____*

Food_____

_____

Drinks_____

Supplements/Medications

How many servings of vegetables did you eat today?

How many glasses of water did you drink today?

Exercise:

Mindfulness & Meditation:

Personal Activities:

What 3 things are you grateful for today?

1.

2.

3.

What could you have done better today?

DATE: /   / 20

How are you feeling today?

                    Urgh   OK   Good   Fantastic

How did you sleep last night?

_____

Breakfast   *Time_____*

Food_____

_____

_____

Drinks_____

Lunch   *Time_____*

Food_____

_____

_____

Drinks_____

Dinner   *Time_____*

Food_____

_____

_____

Drinks_____

Snacks   *Time_____*

Food_____

_____

_____

Drinks_____

Supplements/Medications

_____

How many servings of vegetables did you eat today?

_____

How many glasses of water did you drink today?

_____

Exercise:

_____

_____

Mindfulness & Meditation:

_____

_____

Personal Activities:

_____

_____

What 3 things are you grateful for today?

1._____
2._____
3._____

What could you have done better today?

_____

_____

_____

DATE: /   / 20

How are you feeling today?

                Urgh   OK   Good   Fantastic

How did you sleep last night?

_____

Breakfast   *Time*_____

*Food*_____

_____

_____

*Drinks*_____

Lunch   *Time*_____

*Food*_____

_____

_____

*Drinks*_____

Dinner   *Time*_____

*Food*_____

_____

_____

*Drinks*_____

Snacks   *Time*_____

*Food*_____

_____

_____

*Drinks*_____

Supplements/Medications

How many servings of vegetables did you eat today?

How many glasses of water did you drink today?

Exercise:

Mindfulness & Meditation:

Personal Activities:

What 3 things are you grateful for today?

1.

2.

3.

What could you have done better today?

DATE: /   / 20

How are you feeling today?

                Urgh   OK   Good   Fantastic

How did you sleep last night?

_____

Breakfast   *Time_____*

Food_____

_____

Drinks_____

Lunch   *Time_____*

Food_____

_____

Drinks_____

Dinner   *Time_____*

Food_____

_____

Drinks_____

Snacks   *Time_____*

Food_____

_____

Drinks_____

Supplements/Medications

How many servings of vegetables did you eat today?

How many glasses of water did you drink today?

Exercise:

Mindfulness & Meditation:

Personal Activities:

What 3 things are you grateful for today?

1.

2.

3.

What could you have done better today?

DATE: /   / 20

How are you feeling today?

             Urgh   OK   Good   Fantastic

How did you sleep last night?

Breakfast   *Time*_____
*Food*_____

_____

*Drinks*_____

Lunch   *Time*_____
*Food*_____

_____

*Drinks*_____

Dinner   *Time*_____
*Food*_____

_____

*Drinks*_____

Snacks   *Time*_____
*Food*_____

_____

*Drinks*_____

Supplements/Medications

How many servings of vegetables did you eat today?

How many glasses of water did you drink today?

Exercise:

Mindfulness & Meditation:

Personal Activities:

What 3 things are you grateful for today?
1.
2.
3.

What could you have done better today?

DATE: /   / 20

How are you feeling today?

        Urgh   OK   Good   Fantastic

How did you sleep last night?

_____

Breakfast   *Time_____*

Food_____

_____

_____

Drinks_____

Lunch   *Time_____*

Food_____

_____

_____

Drinks_____

Dinner   *Time_____*

Food_____

_____

_____

Drinks_____

Snacks   *Time_____*

Food_____

_____

_____

Drinks_____

Supplements/Medications

How many servings of vegetables did you eat today?

How many glasses of water did you drink today?

Exercise:

Mindfulness & Meditation:

Personal Activities:

What 3 things are you grateful for today?

1.

2.

3.

What could you have done better today?

DATE: /   / 20

How are you feeling today?

                Urgh   *OK*   *Good*   *Fantastic*

How did you sleep last night?

_____

Breakfast   *Time_____*

Food_____

_____

Drinks_____

Lunch   *Time_____*

Food_____

_____

Drinks_____

Dinner   *Time_____*

Food_____

_____

Drinks_____

Snacks   *Time_____*

Food_____

_____

Drinks_____

Supplements/Medications

How many servings of vegetables did you eat today?

How many glasses of water did you drink today?

Exercise:

Mindfulness & Meditation:

Personal Activities:

What 3 things are you grateful for today?

1.

2.

3.

What could you have done better today?

DATE: /   / 20

How are you feeling today?

         Urgh   *OK*   *Good*   *Fantastic*

How did you sleep last night?

_____

Breakfast   *Time_____*

Food_____

_____

Drinks_____

Lunch   *Time_____*

Food_____

_____

Drinks_____

Dinner   *Time_____*

Food_____

_____

Drinks_____

Snacks   *Time_____*

Food_____

_____

Drinks_____

Supplements/Medications

_____

How many servings of vegetables did you eat today?

_____

How many glasses of water did you drink today?

_____

Exercise:

_____

_____

Mindfulness & Meditation:

_____

_____

Personal Activities:

_____

_____

What 3 things are you grateful for today?

1._____

2._____

3._____

What could you have done better today?

_____

_____

_____

DATE: /   / 20

How are you feeling today?

        Urgh   *OK*   *Good*   *Fantastic*

How did you sleep last night?

_____

Breakfast   *Time_____*

Food_____

_____

Drinks_____

Lunch   *Time_____*

Food_____

_____

Drinks_____

Dinner   *Time_____*

Food_____

_____

Drinks_____

Snacks   *Time_____*

Food_____

_____

Drinks_____

Supplements/Medications

_____

How many servings of vegetables did you eat today?

_____

How many glasses of water did you drink today?

_____

Exercise:

_____
_____

Mindfulness & Meditation:

_____
_____

Personal Activities:

_____
_____

What 3 things are you grateful for today?
1._____
2._____
3._____

What could you have done better today?

_____
_____
_____

DATE: / / 20

How are you feeling today?

        Urgh   *OK*   *Good*   *Fantastic*

How did you sleep last night?

_____

Breakfast   *Time_____*

Food_____

_____

_____

Drinks_____

Lunch   *Time_____*

Food_____

_____

_____

Drinks_____

Dinner   *Time_____*

Food_____

_____

_____

Drinks_____

Snacks   *Time_____*

Food_____

_____

_____

Drinks_____

Supplements/Medications

_____

How many servings of vegetables did you eat today?

_____

How many glasses of water did you drink today?

_____

Exercise:

_____

_____

Mindfulness & Meditation:

_____

_____

Personal Activities:

_____

_____

What 3 things are you grateful for today?

1._____

2._____

3._____

What could you have done better today?

_____

_____

_____

DATE: / / 20

How are you feeling today?

Urgh   OK   Good   Fantastic

How did you sleep last night?

_____

Breakfast   *Time_____*

Food_____

_____

_____

Drinks_____

Lunch   *Time_____*

Food_____

_____

_____

Drinks_____

Dinner   *Time_____*

Food_____

_____

_____

Drinks_____

Snacks   *Time_____*

Food_____

_____

_____

Drinks_____

Supplements/Medications

_____

How many servings of vegetables did you eat today?

_____

How many glasses of water did you drink today?

_____

Exercise:

_____

_____

Mindfulness & Meditation:

_____

_____

Personal Activities:

_____

_____

What 3 things are you grateful for today?

1._____
2._____
3._____

What could you have done better today?

_____

_____

_____

DATE: / / 20

How are you feeling today?

Urgh   OK   Good   Fantastic

How did you sleep last night?

_____

Breakfast   *Time_____*

Food_____

_____

_____

Drinks_____

Lunch   *Time_____*

Food_____

_____

_____

Drinks_____

Dinner   *Time_____*

Food_____

_____

_____

Drinks_____

Snacks   *Time_____*

Food_____

_____

_____

Drinks_____

Supplements/Medications

_____

How many servings of vegetables did you eat today?

_____

How many glasses of water did you drink today?

_____

Exercise:

_____

_____

Mindfulness & Meditation:

_____

_____

Personal Activities:

_____

_____

What 3 things are you grateful for today?

1._____

2._____

3._____

What could you have done better today?

_____

_____

_____

DATE: /   / 20

How are you feeling today?

               Urgh   OK   Good   Fantastic

How did you sleep last night?

_____

Breakfast   *Time_____*

Food_____

_____

_____

Drinks_____

Lunch   *Time_____*

Food_____

_____

_____

Drinks_____

Dinner   *Time_____*

Food_____

_____

_____

Drinks_____

Snacks   *Time_____*

Food_____

_____

_____

Drinks_____

Supplements/Medications

How many servings of vegetables did you eat today?

How many glasses of water did you drink today?

Exercise:

Mindfulness & Meditation:

Personal Activities:

What 3 things are you grateful for today?

1.

2.

3.

What could you have done better today?

DATE: / / 20

How are you feeling today?

        Urgh   OK   Good   Fantastic

How did you sleep last night?

_____

Breakfast   *Time*_____

*Food*_____

_____

_____

*Drinks*_____

Lunch   *Time*_____

*Food*_____

_____

_____

*Drinks*_____

Dinner   *Time*_____

*Food*_____

_____

_____

*Drinks*_____

Snacks   *Time*_____

*Food*_____

_____

_____

*Drinks*_____

Supplements/Medications

How many servings of vegetables did you eat today?

How many glasses of water did you drink today?

Exercise:

Mindfulness & Meditation:

Personal Activities:

What 3 things are you grateful for today?

1._____

2._____

3._____

What could you have done better today?

How are you feeling today?

                     Urgh   OK   Good   Fantastic

How did you sleep last night?

_____

Breakfast　　　*Time_____*

Food_____

_____

Drinks_____

Lunch　　　*Time_____*

Food_____

_____

Drinks_____

Dinner　　　*Time_____*

Food_____

_____

Drinks_____

Snacks　　　*Time_____*

Food_____

_____

Drinks_____

Supplements/Medications

_____

How many servings of vegetables did you eat today?

_____

How many glasses of water did you drink today?

_____

Exercise:

_____

_____

Mindfulness & Meditation:

_____

_____

Personal Activities:

_____

_____

What 3 things are you grateful for today?

1._____

2._____

3._____

What could you have done better today?

_____

_____

_____

DATE: /   / 20

How are you feeling today?

Urgh   OK   Good   Fantastic

How did you sleep last night?

_____

Breakfast   *Time_____*

Food_____

_____

Drinks_____

Lunch   *Time_____*

Food_____

_____

Drinks_____

Dinner   *Time_____*

Food_____

_____

Drinks_____

Snacks   *Time_____*

Food_____

_____

Drinks_____

Supplements/Medications

_____

How many servings of vegetables did you eat today?

_____

How many glasses of water did you drink today?

_____

Exercise:

_____

_____

Mindfulness & Meditation:

_____

_____

Personal Activities:

_____

_____

What 3 things are you grateful for today?

1._____
2._____
3._____

What could you have done better today?

_____

_____

_____

DATE: /   / 20

How are you feeling today?

Urgh   OK   Good   Fantastic

How did you sleep last night?

_____

Breakfast   *Time_____*

*Food*_____

_____

_____

*Drinks*_____

Lunch   *Time_____*

*Food*_____

_____

_____

*Drinks*_____

Dinner   *Time_____*

*Food*_____

_____

_____

*Drinks*_____

Snacks   *Time_____*

*Food*_____

_____

_____

*Drinks*_____

Supplements/Medications

How many servings of vegetables did you eat today?

How many glasses of water did you drink today?

Exercise:

Mindfulness & Meditation:

Personal Activities:

What 3 things are you grateful for today?
1.
2.
3.

What could you have done better today?

DATE: /   / 20

How are you feeling today?

Urgh   OK   Good   Fantastic

How did you sleep last night?

_____

Breakfast   *Time_____*

Food_____

_____

_____

Drinks_____

Lunch   *Time_____*

Food_____

_____

_____

Drinks_____

Dinner   *Time_____*

Food_____

_____

_____

Drinks_____

Snacks   *Time_____*

Food_____

_____

_____

Drinks_____

Supplements/Medications

_____

How many servings of vegetables did you eat today?

_____

How many glasses of water did you drink today?

_____

Exercise:

_____

_____

Mindfulness & Meditation:

_____

_____

Personal Activities:

_____

_____

What 3 things are you grateful for today?

1._____
2._____
3._____

What could you have done better today?

_____

_____

_____

DATE: /   / 20

How are you feeling today?

     Urgh OK Good Fantastic

How did you sleep last night?

_____

Breakfast *Time_____*

Food_____

_____

_____

Drinks_____

Lunch   *Time_____*

Food_____

_____

_____

Drinks_____

Dinner   *Time_____*

Food_____

_____

_____

Drinks_____

Snacks   *Time_____*

Food_____

_____

_____

Drinks_____

Supplements/Medications

_____

How many servings of vegetables did you eat today?

_____

How many glasses of water did you drink today?

_____

Exercise:

_____

_____

Mindfulness & Meditation:

_____

_____

Personal Activities:

_____

_____

What 3 things are you grateful for today?

1._____
2._____
3._____

What could you have done better today?

_____

_____

_____

DATE: /   / 20

How are you feeling today?

                Urgh   *OK*   *Good*   *Fantastic*

How did you sleep last night?

_____

Breakfast   *Time_____*

Food_____

_____

Drinks_____

Lunch   *Time_____*

Food_____

_____

Drinks_____

Dinner   *Time_____*

Food_____

_____

Drinks_____

Snacks   *Time_____*

Food_____

_____

Drinks_____

Supplements/Medications

_____

How many servings of vegetables did you eat today?

_____

How many glasses of water did you drink today?

_____

Exercise:

_____

_____

Mindfulness & Meditation:

_____

_____

Personal Activities:

_____

_____

What 3 things are you grateful for today?

1._____

2._____

3._____

What could you have done better today?

_____

_____

_____

How are you feeling today?

        Urgh   *OK*   *Good*   *Fantastic*

How did you sleep last night?

_____

Breakfast   *Time_____*

Food_____

_____

Drinks_____

Lunch   *Time_____*

Food_____

_____

Drinks_____

Dinner   *Time_____*

Food_____

_____

Drinks_____

Snacks   *Time_____*

Food_____

_____

Drinks_____

Supplements/Medications

_____

How many servings of vegetables did you eat today?

_____

How many glasses of water did you drink today?

_____

Exercise:

_____

_____

Mindfulness & Meditation:

_____

_____

Personal Activities:

_____

_____

What 3 things are you grateful for today?

1._____

2._____

3._____

What could you have done better today?

_____

_____

_____

DATE: /   / 20

How are you feeling today?

Urgh   OK   Good   Fantastic

How did you sleep last night?

_____

Breakfast   *Time*_____

*Food*_____

_____

_____

*Drinks*_____

Lunch   *Time*_____

*Food*_____

_____

_____

*Drinks*_____

Dinner   *Time*_____

*Food*_____

_____

_____

*Drinks*_____

Snacks   *Time*_____

*Food*_____

_____

_____

*Drinks*_____

Supplements/Medications

_____

How many servings of vegetables did you eat today?

_____

How many glasses of water did you drink today?

_____

Exercise:

_____

_____

Mindfulness & Meditation:

_____

_____

Personal Activities:

_____

_____

What 3 things are you grateful for today?

1._____

2._____

3._____

What could you have done better today?

_____

_____

_____

DATE: / / 20

How are you feeling today?

Urgh   OK   Good   Fantastic

How did you sleep last night?

_____

Breakfast   *Time_____*

Food_____

_____

_____

Drinks_____

Lunch   *Time_____*

Food_____

_____

_____

Drinks_____

Dinner   *Time_____*

Food_____

_____

_____

Drinks_____

Snacks   *Time_____*

Food_____

_____

_____

Drinks_____

Supplements/Medications

How many servings of vegetables did you eat today?

How many glasses of water did you drink today?

Exercise:

Mindfulness & Meditation:

Personal Activities:

What 3 things are you grateful for today?

1.

2.

3.

What could you have done better today?

DATE: /   / 20

How are you feeling today?

                  Urgh   OK   Good   Fantastic

How did you sleep last night?

_____

Breakfast   *Time_____*

Food_____

_____

Drinks_____

Lunch   *Time_____*

Food_____

_____

Drinks_____

Dinner   *Time_____*

Food_____

_____

Drinks_____

Snacks   *Time_____*

Food_____

_____

Drinks_____

Supplements/Medications

_____

How many servings of vegetables did you eat today?

_____

How many glasses of water did you drink today?

_____

Exercise:

_____

_____

Mindfulness & Meditation:

_____

_____

Personal Activities:

_____

_____

What 3 things are you grateful for today?

1._____

2._____

3._____

What could you have done better today?

_____

_____

_____

DATE: /   / 20

How are you feeling today?

        Urgh   *OK*   *Good*   *Fantastic*

How did you sleep last night?

_____

Breakfast   *Time_____*

Food_____

_____

_____

Drinks_____

Lunch   *Time_____*

Food_____

_____

_____

Drinks_____

Dinner   *Time_____*

Food_____

_____

_____

Drinks_____

Snacks   *Time_____*

Food_____

_____

_____

Drinks_____

Supplements/Medications

How many servings of vegetables did you eat today?

How many glasses of water did you drink today?

Exercise:

Mindfulness & Meditation:

Personal Activities:

What 3 things are you grateful for today?

1.

2.

3.

What could you have done better today?

DATE: /   / 20

How are you feeling today?

        Urgh   *OK*   *Good*   *Fantastic*

How did you sleep last night?

_____

Breakfast   *Time_____*

Food_____

_____

Drinks_____

Lunch   *Time_____*

Food_____

_____

Drinks_____

Dinner   *Time_____*

Food_____

_____

Drinks_____

Snacks   *Time_____*

Food_____

_____

Drinks_____

Supplements/Medications

How many servings of vegetables did you eat today?

How many glasses of water did you drink today?

Exercise:

Mindfulness & Meditation:

Personal Activities:

What 3 things are you grateful for today?

1.

2.

3.

What could you have done better today?

DATE: /   / 20

How are you feeling today?

Urgh   OK   Good   Fantastic

How did you sleep last night?

_____

Breakfast   *Time*_____
*Food*_____
_____
_____
*Drinks*_____

Lunch   *Time*_____
*Food*_____
_____
_____
*Drinks*_____

Dinner   *Time*_____
*Food*_____
_____
_____
*Drinks*_____

Snacks   *Time*_____
*Food*_____
_____
_____
*Drinks*_____

Supplements/Medications

_____

How many servings of vegetables did you eat today?

_____

How many glasses of water did you drink today?

_____

Exercise:

_____

_____

Mindfulness & Meditation:

_____

_____

Personal Activities:

_____

_____

What 3 things are you grateful for today?

1._____

2._____

3._____

What could you have done better today?

_____

_____

_____

DATE: /   / 20

How are you feeling today?

Urgh   OK   Good   Fantastic

How did you sleep last night?

_____

Breakfast   *Time_____*

Food_____

_____

_____

Drinks_____

Lunch   *Time_____*

Food_____

_____

_____

Drinks_____

Dinner   *Time_____*

Food_____

_____

_____

Drinks_____

Snacks   *Time_____*

Food_____

_____

_____

Drinks_____

Supplements/Medications

_____

How many servings of vegetables did you eat today?

_____

How many glasses of water did you drink today?

_____

Exercise:

_____

_____

Mindfulness & Meditation:

_____

_____

Personal Activities:

_____

_____

What 3 things are you grateful for today?

1._____

2._____

3._____

What could you have done better today?

_____

_____

_____

DATE: / / 20

How are you feeling today?

Urgh   OK   Good   Fantastic

How did you sleep last night?

_____

Breakfast   *Time*_____

*Food*_____

_____

_____

*Drinks*_____

Lunch   *Time*_____

*Food*_____

_____

_____

*Drinks*_____

Dinner   *Time*_____

*Food*_____

_____

_____

*Drinks*_____

Snacks   *Time*_____

*Food*_____

_____

_____

*Drinks*_____

Supplements/Medications

_____

How many servings of vegetables did you eat today?

_____

How many glasses of water did you drink today?

_____

Exercise:

_____

_____

Mindfulness & Meditation:

_____

_____

Personal Activities:

_____

_____

What 3 things are you grateful for today?

1._____

2._____

3._____

What could you have done better today?

_____

_____

_____

DATE: /   / 20

How are you feeling today?

        Urgh   *OK*   *Good*   *Fantastic*

How did you sleep last night?

_____

Breakfast   *Time_____*

Food_____

_____

_____

Drinks_____

Lunch   *Time_____*

Food_____

_____

_____

Drinks_____

Dinner   *Time_____*

Food_____

_____

_____

Drinks_____

Snacks   *Time_____*

Food_____

_____

_____

Drinks_____

Supplements/Medications

How many servings of vegetables did you eat today?

How many glasses of water did you drink today?

Exercise:

Mindfulness & Meditation:

Personal Activities:

What 3 things are you grateful for today?

1.

2.

3.

What could you have done better today?

DATE: /   / 20

How are you feeling today?

Urgh   OK   Good   Fantastic

How did you sleep last night?

_____

Breakfast   *Time*_____
*Food*_____
_____
_____
*Drinks*_____

Lunch   *Time*_____
*Food*_____
_____
_____
*Drinks*_____

Dinner   *Time*_____
*Food*_____
_____
_____
*Drinks*_____

Snacks   *Time*_____
*Food*_____
_____
_____
*Drinks*_____

Supplements/Medications

_____

How many servings of vegetables did you eat today?

_____

How many glasses of water did you drink today?

_____

Exercise:

_____

_____

Mindfulness & Meditation:

_____

_____

Personal Activities:

_____

_____

What 3 things are you grateful for today?

1._____

2._____

3._____

What could you have done better today?

_____

_____

_____

DATE: /   / 20

How are you feeling today?

 Urgh   OK   Good   Fantastic

How did you sleep last night?

_____

Breakfast   *Time_____*

Food_____

_____

_____

Drinks_____

Lunch   *Time_____*

Food_____

_____

_____

Drinks_____

Dinner   *Time_____*

Food_____

_____

_____

Drinks_____

Snacks   *Time_____*

Food_____

_____

_____

Drinks_____

Supplements/Medications

_____

How many servings of vegetables did you eat today?

_____

How many glasses of water did you drink today?

_____

Exercise:

_____

_____

Mindfulness & Meditation:

_____

_____

Personal Activities:

_____

_____

What 3 things are you grateful for today?
1._____
2._____
3._____

What could you have done better today?

_____

_____

_____

DATE: /   / 20

How are you feeling today?

                    Urgh   *OK*   *Good*   *Fantastic*

How did you sleep last night?

_____

Breakfast   *Time_____*

Food_____

_____

_____

Drinks_____

Lunch   *Time_____*

Food_____

_____

_____

Drinks_____

Dinner   *Time_____*

Food_____

_____

_____

Drinks_____

Snacks   *Time_____*

Food_____

_____

_____

Drinks_____

Supplements/Medications

How many servings of vegetables did you eat today?

How many glasses of water did you drink today?

Exercise:

Mindfulness & Meditation:

Personal Activities:

What 3 things are you grateful for today?

1.

2.

3.

What could you have done better today?

DATE: /   / 20

How are you feeling today?

               Urgh   OK   Good   Fantastic

How did you sleep last night?

_____

Breakfast   *Time_____*

Food_____

_____

_____

Drinks_____

Lunch   *Time_____*

Food_____

_____

_____

Drinks_____

Dinner   *Time_____*

Food_____

_____

_____

Drinks_____

Snacks   *Time_____*

Food_____

_____

_____

Drinks_____

Supplements/Medications

How many servings of vegetables did you eat today?

How many glasses of water did you drink today?

Exercise:

Mindfulness & Meditation:

Personal Activities:

What 3 things are you grateful for today?

1.

2.

3.

What could you have done better today?

DATE: /   / 20

How are you feeling today?

Urgh   OK   Good   Fantastic

How did you sleep last night?

_____

Breakfast   *Time_____*
Food_____
_____
_____
Drinks_____

Lunch   *Time_____*
Food_____
_____
_____
Drinks_____

Dinner   *Time_____*
Food_____
_____
_____
Drinks_____

Snacks   *Time_____*
Food_____
_____
_____
Drinks_____

Supplements/Medications

_____

How many servings of vegetables did you eat today?

_____

How many glasses of water did you drink today?

_____

Exercise:

_____

_____

Mindfulness & Meditation:

_____

_____

Personal Activities:

_____

_____

What 3 things are you grateful for today?

1._____

2._____

3._____

What could you have done better today?

_____

_____

_____

DATE: /   / 20

How are you feeling today?

               Urgh   *OK*   *Good*   *Fantastic*

How did you sleep last night?

_____

Breakfast   *Time*_____

*Food*_____

_____

*Drinks*_____

Lunch   *Time*_____

*Food*_____

_____

*Drinks*_____

Dinner   *Time*_____

*Food*_____

_____

*Drinks*_____

Snacks   *Time*_____

*Food*_____

_____

*Drinks*_____

Supplements/Medications

_____

How many servings of vegetables did you eat today?

_____

How many glasses of water did you drink today?

_____

Exercise:

_____

_____

Mindfulness & Meditation:

_____

_____

Personal Activities:

_____

_____

What 3 things are you grateful for today?

1._____

2._____

3._____

What could you have done better today?

_____

_____

_____

DATE: /   / 20

How are you feeling today?

        Urgh   OK   Good   Fantastic

How did you sleep last night?

_____

Breakfast   *Time_____*

Food_____

_____

Drinks_____

Lunch   *Time_____*

Food_____

_____

Drinks_____

Dinner   *Time_____*

Food_____

_____

Drinks_____

Snacks   *Time_____*

Food_____

_____

Drinks_____

Supplements/Medications

_____

How many servings of vegetables did you eat today?

_____

How many glasses of water did you drink today?

_____

Exercise:

_____

_____

Mindfulness & Meditation:

_____

_____

Personal Activities:

_____

_____

What 3 things are you grateful for today?

1._____

2._____

3._____

What could you have done better today?

_____

_____

_____

DATE: /   / 20

How are you feeling today?

Urgh   OK   Good   Fantastic

How did you sleep last night?

_____

Breakfast   *Time*_____

*Food*_____

_____

_____

*Drinks*_____

Lunch   *Time*_____

*Food*_____

_____

_____

*Drinks*_____

Dinner   *Time*_____

*Food*_____

_____

_____

*Drinks*_____

Snacks   *Time*_____

*Food*_____

_____

_____

*Drinks*_____

Supplements/Medications

_____

How many servings of vegetables did you eat today?

_____

How many glasses of water did you drink today?

_____

Exercise:

_____

_____

Mindfulness & Meditation:

_____

_____

Personal Activities:

_____

_____

What 3 things are you grateful for today?

1._____

2._____

3._____

What could you have done better today?

_____

_____

_____

DATE: /   / 20

How are you feeling today?

                Urgh   *OK*   *Good*   *Fantastic*

How did you sleep last night?

_____

Breakfast   *Time_____*

Food_____

_____

Drinks_____

Lunch   *Time_____*

Food_____

_____

Drinks_____

Dinner   *Time_____*

Food_____

_____

Drinks_____

Snacks   *Time_____*

Food_____

_____

Drinks_____

Supplements/Medications

_____

How many servings of vegetables did you eat today?

_____

How many glasses of water did you drink today?

_____

Exercise:

_____

_____

Mindfulness & Meditation:

_____

_____

Personal Activities:

_____

_____

What 3 things are you grateful for today?

1._____
2._____
3._____

What could you have done better today?

_____

_____

_____

DATE: / / 20

How are you feeling today?

　　　　　　Urgh　　OK　　Good　　Fantastic

How did you sleep last night?

_____

Breakfast　　Time_____

*Food*_____

_____

_____

*Drinks*_____

Lunch　　Time_____

*Food*_____

_____

_____

*Drinks*_____

Dinner　　Time_____

*Food*_____

_____

_____

*Drinks*_____

Snacks　　Time_____

*Food*_____

_____

_____

*Drinks*_____

Supplements/Medications

_____

How many servings of vegetables did you eat today?

_____

How many glasses of water did you drink today?

_____

Exercise:

_____

_____

Mindfulness & Meditation:

_____

_____

Personal Activities:

_____

_____

What 3 things are you grateful for today?

1._____

2._____

3._____

What could you have done better today?

_____

_____

_____

DATE: /   / 20

How are you feeling today?

        Urgh   OK   Good   Fantastic

How did you sleep last night?

_____

Breakfast   *Time*_____

*Food*_____

_____

_____

*Drinks*_____

Lunch   *Time*_____

*Food*_____

_____

_____

*Drinks*_____

Dinner   *Time*_____

*Food*_____

_____

_____

*Drinks*_____

Snacks   *Time*_____

*Food*_____

_____

_____

*Drinks*_____

Supplements/Medications

_____

How many servings of vegetables did you eat today?

_____

How many glasses of water did you drink today?

_____

Exercise:

_____

_____

Mindfulness & Meditation:

_____

_____

Personal Activities:

_____

_____

What 3 things are you grateful for today?

1._____

2._____

3._____

What could you have done better today?

_____

_____

_____

DATE: /   / 20

How are you feeling today?

Urgh   OK   Good   Fantastic

How did you sleep last night?

_____

Breakfast   *Time_____*

Food_____

_____

_____

Drinks_____

Lunch   *Time_____*

Food_____

_____

_____

Drinks_____

Dinner   *Time_____*

Food_____

_____

_____

Drinks_____

Snacks   *Time_____*

Food_____

_____

_____

Drinks_____

Supplements/Medications

_____

How many servings of vegetables did you eat today?

_____

How many glasses of water did you drink today?

_____

Exercise:

_____

_____

Mindfulness & Meditation:

_____

_____

Personal Activities:

_____

_____

What 3 things are you grateful for today?

1._____

2._____

3._____

What could you have done better today?

_____

_____

_____

DATE: /   / 20

How are you feeling today?

                Urgh   OK   Good   Fantastic

How did you sleep last night?

_____

Breakfast   *Time_____*
Food_____
_____
_____
Drinks_____

Lunch   *Time_____*
Food_____
_____
_____
Drinks_____

Dinner   *Time_____*
Food_____
_____
_____
Drinks_____

Snacks   *Time_____*
Food_____
_____
_____
Drinks_____

Supplements/Medications

_____

How many servings of vegetables did you eat today?

_____

How many glasses of water did you drink today?

_____

Exercise:

_____

_____

Mindfulness & Meditation:

_____

_____

Personal Activities:

_____

_____

What 3 things are you grateful for today?

1._____

2._____

3._____

What could you have done better today?

_____

_____

_____

DATE: /   / 20

How are you feeling today?

                 Urgh   *OK*   *Good*   *Fantastic*

How did you sleep last night?

_____

Breakfast   *Time_____*

Food_____

_____

_____

Drinks_____

Lunch   *Time_____*

Food_____

_____

_____

Drinks_____

Dinner   *Time_____*

Food_____

_____

_____

Drinks_____

Snacks   *Time_____*

Food_____

_____

_____

Drinks_____

Supplements/Medications

_____

How many servings of vegetables did you eat today?

_____

How many glasses of water did you drink today?

_____

Exercise:

_____

_____

Mindfulness & Meditation:

_____

_____

Personal Activities:

_____

_____

What 3 things are you grateful for today?

1._____

2._____

3._____

What could you have done better today?

_____

_____

_____

How are you feeling today?

              Urgh   *OK*   *Good*   *Fantastic*

How did you sleep last night?

_____

Breakfast   *Time_____*

Food_____

_____

_____

Drinks_____

Lunch   *Time_____*

Food_____

_____

_____

Drinks_____

Dinner   *Time_____*

Food_____

_____

_____

Drinks_____

Snacks   *Time_____*

Food_____

_____

_____

Drinks_____

Supplements/Medications

_____

How many servings of vegetables did you eat today?

_____

How many glasses of water did you drink today?

_____

Exercise:

_____

_____

Mindfulness & Meditation:

_____

_____

Personal Activities:

_____

_____

What 3 things are you grateful for today?

1._____

2._____

3._____

What could you have done better today?

_____

_____

_____

DATE: /   / 20

How are you feeling today?

        Urgh   OK   Good   Fantastic

How did you sleep last night?

_____

Breakfast   *Time_____*

Food_____

_____

_____

Drinks_____

Lunch   *Time_____*

Food_____

_____

_____

Drinks_____

Dinner   *Time_____*

Food_____

_____

_____

Drinks_____

Snacks   *Time_____*

Food_____

_____

_____

Drinks_____

Supplements/Medications

How many servings of vegetables did you eat today?

How many glasses of water did you drink today?

Exercise:

Mindfulness & Meditation:

Personal Activities:

What 3 things are you grateful for today?
1.
2.
3.

What could you have done better today?

DATE: /   / 20

How are you feeling today?

               Urgh   OK   Good   Fantastic

How did you sleep last night?

_____

Breakfast   *Time_____*

Food_____

_____

_____

Drinks_____

Lunch   *Time_____*

Food_____

_____

_____

Drinks_____

Dinner   *Time_____*

Food_____

_____

_____

Drinks_____

Snacks   *Time_____*

Food_____

_____

_____

Drinks_____

Supplements/Medications

_____

How many servings of vegetables did you eat today?

_____

How many glasses of water did you drink today?

_____

Exercise:

_____

_____

Mindfulness & Meditation:

_____

_____

Personal Activities:

_____

_____

What 3 things are you grateful for today?

1._____

2._____

3._____

What could you have done better today?

_____

_____

_____

DATE: /   / 20

How are you feeling today?

                Urgh   *OK*   *Good*   *Fantastic*

How did you sleep last night?

_____

Breakfast   *Time_____*

Food_____

_____

_____

Drinks_____

Lunch   *Time_____*

Food_____

_____

_____

Drinks_____

Dinner   *Time_____*

Food_____

_____

_____

Drinks_____

Snacks   *Time_____*

Food_____

_____

_____

Drinks_____

Supplements/Medications

_____

How many servings of vegetables did you eat today?

_____

How many glasses of water did you drink today?

_____

Exercise:

_____

_____

Mindfulness & Meditation:

_____

_____

Personal Activities:

_____

_____

What 3 things are you grateful for today?

1._____

2._____

3._____

What could you have done better today?

_____

_____

_____

DATE: / / 20

How are you feeling today?

Urgh   OK   Good   Fantastic

How did you sleep last night?

_____

Breakfast   *Time*_____

*Food*_____

_____

_____

*Drinks*_____

Lunch   *Time*_____

*Food*_____

_____

_____

*Drinks*_____

Dinner   *Time*_____

*Food*_____

_____

_____

*Drinks*_____

Snacks   *Time*_____

*Food*_____

_____

_____

*Drinks*_____

Supplements/Medications

How many servings of vegetables did you eat today?

How many glasses of water did you drink today?

Exercise:

Mindfulness & Meditation:

Personal Activities:

What 3 things are you grateful for today?

1.

2.

3.

What could you have done better today?

DATE: /   / 20

How are you feeling today?

Urgh   OK   Good   Fantastic

How did you sleep last night?

_____

Breakfast   *Time_____*

*Food*_____

_____

_____

*Drinks*_____

Lunch   *Time_____*

*Food*_____

_____

_____

*Drinks*_____

Dinner   *Time_____*

*Food*_____

_____

_____

*Drinks*_____

Snacks   *Time_____*

*Food*_____

_____

_____

*Drinks*_____

Supplements/Medications

_____

How many servings of vegetables did you eat today?

_____

How many glasses of water did you drink today?

_____

Exercise:

_____

_____

Mindfulness & Meditation:

_____

_____

Personal Activities:

_____

_____

What 3 things are you grateful for today?

1._____

2._____

3._____

What could you have done better today?

_____

_____

_____

DATE: /   / 20

How are you feeling today?

                Urgh   *OK*   *Good*   *Fantastic*

How did you sleep last night?

_____

Breakfast   *Time_____*

Food_____

_____

_____

Drinks_____

Lunch   *Time_____*

Food_____

_____

_____

Drinks_____

Dinner   *Time_____*

Food_____

_____

_____

Drinks_____

Snacks   *Time_____*

Food_____

_____

_____

Drinks_____

Supplements/Medications

How many servings of vegetables did you eat today?

How many glasses of water did you drink today?

Exercise:

Mindfulness & Meditation:

Personal Activities:

What 3 things are you grateful for today?

1.

2.

3.

What could you have done better today?

DATE: /   / 20

How are you feeling today?

                Urgh   *OK*   *Good*   *Fantastic*

How did you sleep last night?

_____

Breakfast   *Time_____*

Food_____

_____

_____

Drinks_____

Lunch   *Time_____*

Food_____

_____

_____

Drinks_____

Dinner   *Time_____*

Food_____

_____

_____

Drinks_____

Snacks   *Time_____*

Food_____

_____

_____

Drinks_____

Supplements/Medications

_____

How many servings of vegetables did you eat today?

_____

How many glasses of water did you drink today?

_____

Exercise:

_____

_____

Mindfulness & Meditation:

_____

_____

Personal Activities:

_____

_____

What 3 things are you grateful for today?
1._____
2._____
3._____

What could you have done better today?

_____

_____

_____

DATE: /   / 20

How are you feeling today?

                Urgh   OK   Good   Fantastic

How did you sleep last night?

_____

Breakfast   *Time_____*

Food_____

_____

Drinks_____

Lunch   *Time_____*

Food_____

_____

Drinks_____

Dinner   *Time_____*

Food_____

_____

Drinks_____

Snacks   *Time_____*

Food_____

_____

Drinks_____

Supplements/Medications

_____

How many servings of vegetables did you eat today?

_____

How many glasses of water did you drink today?

_____

Exercise:

_____

_____

Mindfulness & Meditation:

_____

_____

Personal Activities:

_____

_____

What 3 things are you grateful for today?

1._____
2._____
3._____

What could you have done better today?

_____

_____

_____

DATE: /   / 20

How are you feeling today?

Urgh   OK   Good   Fantastic

How did you sleep last night?

_____

Breakfast   *Time_____*

Food_____

_____

_____

Drinks_____

Lunch   *Time_____*

Food_____

_____

_____

Drinks_____

Dinner   *Time_____*

Food_____

_____

_____

Drinks_____

Snacks   *Time_____*

Food_____

_____

_____

Drinks_____

Supplements/Medications

_____

How many servings of vegetables did you eat today?

_____

How many glasses of water did you drink today?

_____

Exercise:

_____

_____

Mindfulness & Meditation:

_____

_____

Personal Activities:

_____

_____

What 3 things are you grateful for today?

1._____

2._____

3._____

What could you have done better today?

_____

_____

_____

DATE: /   / 20

How are you feeling today?

        Urgh   OK   Good   Fantastic

How did you sleep last night?

_____

Breakfast   *Time_____*

Food_____

_____

Drinks_____

Lunch   *Time_____*

Food_____

_____

Drinks_____

Dinner   *Time_____*

Food_____

_____

Drinks_____

Snacks   *Time_____*

Food_____

_____

Drinks_____

Supplements/Medications

_____

How many servings of vegetables did you eat today?

_____

How many glasses of water did you drink today?

_____

Exercise:

_____

_____

Mindfulness & Meditation:

_____

_____

Personal Activities:

_____

_____

What 3 things are you grateful for today?

1._____

2._____

3._____

What could you have done better today?

_____

_____

_____

DATE: /   / 20

How are you feeling today?

               Urgh   *OK*   *Good*   *Fantastic*

How did you sleep last night?

_____

Breakfast   *Time_____*

Food_____

_____

_____

Drinks_____

Lunch   *Time_____*

Food_____

_____

_____

Drinks_____

Dinner   *Time_____*

Food_____

_____

_____

Drinks_____

Snacks   *Time_____*

Food_____

_____

_____

Drinks_____

Supplements/Medications

_____

How many servings of vegetables did you eat today?

_____

How many glasses of water did you drink today?

_____

Exercise:

_____

_____

Mindfulness & Meditation:

_____

_____

Personal Activities:

_____

_____

What 3 things are you grateful for today?

1._____

2._____

3._____

What could you have done better today?

_____

_____

_____

DATE: /   / 20

How are you feeling today?

Urgh   OK   Good   Fantastic

How did you sleep last night?

_____

Breakfast   *Time_____*

Food_____

_____

_____

Drinks_____

Lunch   *Time_____*

Food_____

_____

_____

Drinks_____

Dinner   *Time_____*

Food_____

_____

_____

Drinks_____

Snacks   *Time_____*

Food_____

_____

_____

Drinks_____

Supplements/Medications

How many servings of vegetables did you eat today?

How many glasses of water did you drink today?

Exercise:

Mindfulness & Meditation:

Personal Activities:

What 3 things are you grateful for today?

1.

2.

3.

What could you have done better today?

DATE: /   / 20

How are you feeling today?

        Urgh   *OK*   *Good*   *Fantastic*

How did you sleep last night?

_____

Breakfast   *Time_____*

Food_____

_____

_____

Drinks_____

Lunch   *Time_____*

Food_____

_____

_____

Drinks_____

Dinner   *Time_____*

Food_____

_____

_____

Drinks_____

Snacks   *Time_____*

Food_____

_____

_____

Drinks_____

Supplements/Medications

_____

How many servings of vegetables did you eat today?

_____

How many glasses of water did you drink today?

_____

Exercise:

_____

_____

Mindfulness & Meditation:

_____

_____

Personal Activities:

_____

_____

What 3 things are you grateful for today?

1._____

2._____

3._____

What could you have done better today?

_____

_____

_____

DATE: /   / 20

How are you feeling today?

        Urgh   *OK*   *Good*   *Fantastic*

How did you sleep last night?

_____

Breakfast   *Time_____*

Food_____

_____

_____

Drinks_____

Lunch   *Time_____*

Food_____

_____

_____

Drinks_____

Dinner   *Time_____*

Food_____

_____

_____

Drinks_____

Snacks   *Time_____*

Food_____

_____

_____

Drinks_____

Supplements/Medications

How many servings of vegetables did you eat today?

How many glasses of water did you drink today?

Exercise:

Mindfulness & Meditation:

Personal Activities:

What 3 things are you grateful for today?

1.

2.

3.

What could you have done better today?

How are you feeling today?

Urgh   OK   Good   Fantastic

How did you sleep last night?

_____

Breakfast   *Time*_____

*Food*_____

_____

_____

*Drinks*_____

Lunch   *Time*_____

*Food*_____

_____

_____

*Drinks*_____

Dinner   *Time*_____

*Food*_____

_____

_____

*Drinks*_____

Snacks   *Time*_____

*Food*_____

_____

_____

*Drinks*_____

Supplements/Medications

_____

How many servings of vegetables did you eat today?

_____

How many glasses of water did you drink today?

_____

Exercise:

_____

_____

Mindfulness & Meditation:

_____

_____

Personal Activities:

_____

_____

What 3 things are you grateful for today?

1._____

2._____

3._____

What could you have done better today?

_____

_____

_____

Printed in Great Britain
by Amazon